# Drift Gestures

# Drift Gestures

*poems*

C. S. MILLS

*Drift Gestures: Poems*
First Edition

ISBN 978-1-7328741-6-9
Library of Congress Control Number: 2023946735

Cover art by Indigo Deany
Printed in the United States of America

The Lune
Fort Collins, CO
www.poetsonearth.com

*for my mother,*
*SJM*

*Rising water*

For souls, death is to become water; and death
for water to become earth; and from earth
comes water; and from water, soul.


HERACLITUS

# Invocation

Rise cold water. Rise to the
knees, to the hands, to the belly.
Rise and envelop the body.

What does the body feel?
Cold. *Beloved body, beloved cold.*
What does the body fear?
Death. *Beloved fear, beloved death.*
Are we ready? No, *we are not ready.*
No-ready.

We are not ready but the water rises.
*Beloved teacher, beloved messenger.*
Answer with a shaky laugh
as the initiatory water rises:

*Yes! we are not ready.*
Whatever to come
asks we not be ready.

⁜

Across the threshold mind-body unfurl.
No longer hand but sprouts around a
stump, not eye but lightless antichthon,
not tooth but arc of luminous spiral;
not flesh but deepest muck.

Not breath but a knot in the air,
no life but amidst death. Not death
but a body of cold water.

⁜

Prepare the mineral bowl.
Cast the circle, flood the center,
follow circumference until
a subtle harmonic rises
oblique to the rim.

Finally, loose the knot.
Hold strands amid sprouts
dancing in the wind
—swim through.

Three visitings

*One*
At the height of the longest day, against silica sky over
the island there comes a puzzling sign. It is a ring of
vapor described by glinting cruciform craft whose white
plumage hides beneath a thin osmium carapace. Ring
morphs to isometric helix to icedust wingsweep—the
craft likely a visiting from some peri-modern Atlantean
people, a projection from that present-future-primeval
unconscious beneath the azure swell.

Possibly to remind us:
That there rose a golden dome from the Aegean plane,
rose atop ash-white stone walls dutifully limewashed
blank, blank yet charged numinous by slanting shadow
at noon. Recall that beneath the footings there was a
crater lined meticulously with soft white stones. A nest
beneath a temple, remember.

*Two*
The island is ringed at the shore by a low battlement of
branches and boles woven by surf, which at pains we
might dismantle and stack into a stout pyre, which when
lit burns with disquieting rapidity and heat—the faintest
spark encouraged by many hands shall become a great
unholy cleansing conflagration that even the revelers
privately fear. What power is this among our hands?

Step away for a moment, out beyond the battlement,
beyond the glow of the flames, into the moonless night
where the amphibian chorus rises in veils from amid the
reeds. Where at the shore wave laps sand in perennial
wingwash flutter—water stone together the infinitely
self-transforming complexifier.


*Three*
At sunrise endless ponderous lavender glass to the
horizon. From over open water, emerald ball of energy
speeds along elastic catenary to a point before the heart,
heart jumps at the surprise. A fierce weariness, finest
feathers disheveled. *Joy*, says the emerald bird, *joy to
you, we've won*. Tiny precious heart still in the breast,
in two hands cupped.

Venus in Scorpio

At sunset,
Vesper settles
with charged mineral dust
into the ten petals
of the pentagram.

After dark,
Antares keels along its low arc
through the zodiacal stream,
arc a segment of a great ellipse the
    mind follows to hubris;
but hubris admonished
by glistening jointed legs
breaching the horizon.

Along the arc,
four hands clasped
and two bodies orbit one another;
they describe
two overlapping ellipses with
    lens held between.

And around the pentagram,
the twins
Lucifer and Vesper
    never meet,
as if two faces of one body.

One appears
to us as two,
two as one,
—and thus:

In dream,
heart occulted by chitinous plate,
starlit scorpion comes
fast clicking over rocks as
    we fumble backward away.

And above,
through the thin smoke-opal shell
    of the sky,
—an apparition:

Lucifer in delicate crescent;
soft amniotic glow to the cusp an
    ashen light enveloping the sphere.

Twins together there
in the warm vessel.

# Evocation

Lift just one bone
from the mineral body. And
then some blood in a wooden
vessel over the water.

Lift vessel and carry bone
so at the shore we might see
a god rise light in our image
from the crucible.

Lift light image! But god
ever a tricky confluence
eddying dispassionately
onward.

# Five of Cups

Form a brick from the blood-soaked sand,
build a tower that memory cannot climb
in which to admire the sharpness of a spear;
four points to the wind.

See rise from the water the Unholy Heavenly,
that generous killer of kings who patiently,
without passion or malice, will pull down tower
and wear brick back to sand raked in the waves.

Look, five vessels:
One for each known petal of the pentagram,
one for each ritual loop as She circles the tower;
three empty but two withheld.

## Point quincunx



In storm the impenetrable
wholeness of the point unfolds to
four. Merciful. For the human mind has
no means by which to grasp wholeness.

First earth, that mineral body
draped thin over scoured rock.
Flesh and blood thinner yet but
growing. Held to bone at the shore.

Second air:
carry feather, carried by wing.
Pull wave up to charging and
push blade to sand.

Third fire, defeated by wave in storm. Remnant
of the martian tower worn to smooth phallus shrunken
lost in the surf. But fire survives yet when waves
calm. And remnant dry under siege of sun.

And fourth water, that
ineluctable current carry-
ing warmth and cold,
vessel and stone.

Water the agent, excavator, architect and
executor. Who decides by evasion, decides
by scorn. Whose laugh a dispassionate laugh as
it rises in proportion to the panic of our treading.

Water solves, waves give then
take. And in the rise and fall
memory is pumped
onto thirsty earth.

In storm the one unfolds to four, four folds
to three, and three is just two joined by rising water.
Which again calms. And the two settle into
one beneath the cold lens.

# Dilation

Raise them from the still surface,
these hands from the cold lens;

two hands cupped holding
just a little water.

Come here repent. For the
loosing of breath's knot;

spear released
into still air.

For admiring that arc
from these hands.

⁜

But here: heat to
water, cold to blood.
A helical pattern

in the scattering swirl.
Just a little heat to give away,
endless cold to receive.

And yes cold is given too.
Neither breath nor spearthrust
now, but surrender.

Raise these hands to the mouth;
the spring gives some
and withholds some.

*Drift body*

What was scattered
gathers.
What was gathered
blows apart.


HERACLITUS

## Emptying



Drift is the body
of a dismembered god
laid out on bedrock:

scattered gravel    scattered
sand    silt    dust        clay
and crushed bone

    In the body
    darkness enwraps
    the sacred things

All-Mineral
    scattered god

       glacier

whose
memory empties to drift
and

    wells in
    places still
    now.

Yes      Ice empties
to moraine and kettle
      (as wind to dune
                  wave to shore)

Then     only empty    can mineral
know
soil
            fiber
                        flesh

Only can an empty vessel
gather       only can
a scattered body
take shape

Only in
disintegration
persistence


                              ⌗



A god so
drawn to flesh as to
let memory melt
to drift

Flesh
      that breath
              to mineral

⁜

Wind flows over
land      blooms over
moraine      eddies in
valley

        breath in
        the body

Wind mirrors and distorts
both
moraine and
valley overhead

a projection
both
        familiar and un-
        familiar

Grasp land and pull
to resemble bloom or
eddy      and see
projection grow

only
ever more unfamiliar
        ahead
            of our grasp

Bloom of wind over
stone inverts to eddy
in hollow of sand

hand    both
convex and concave
    depending
    on gesture

We grasp at
something grasping
drives away



✢

Each
a beckoning wound
in the body beneath

Six lines up
from the ground
to that silent
hovering
haecceity

A generative grammar


1


rise and walk to the point
where two currents meet,

one from around each shore,
to shape finite sand and stone

into infinite, continuous
forms while the body sleeps.

wake to find them ever more
familiar, but abidingly new.

2

the point speaks, plainly,
in natural numbers:

one vertex, two currents,
three faces, four winds.

speech plain but looping; all-
number, all-image, ceaseless.


3

what counts but is un-
countable? spars but

is unsparing, surfaces
but is non-orientable?


4

rise and walk to the point
where opposites may join.

Harvester one: tern

at noon:
a winged figure glides and cuts across wind off the left-
hand shore, turns and passes twice. attention down

through cold water
passing to blindness
beneath the waves.

to the right the chorus, vociferous from foredune, calls:

*see?*

an angel, messenger, harvester. searching
on two articulated blades shadowed to
the tip, tip shears billowing mass

to line. spearpoint of molten basalt held hungry ahead,
searching. scythe-wings working, tektite eyes alive.

*we see.*

beneath wave a glint of sun
off silver side of elongated disc
spiraling through cold water.

disc dense and keeled, tooled, silver-scaled. crest of spiral
glint scaleshine skyward in silver signal of flesh and breath,

crescent call

*pick me! pick me!*

sicklewing pull to parachute and hover
holding angel overhead. stationary,
preparing for fold to dive, when

tensegrity of bone and ligament light treading wind

transform quick
to dart of lead.

*we. we see!*

hyperbolic plunge. startling
plumb to water to beckoning
scaleshine beneath; air to

water to silver disc.

angel emerge again grasping disc in split spear, shake water
from feathers. disc a beating crescent before pumping wings.

*we.*

yes:
one magmatic spearbill cool and fracture
to two shadowtip wings. plumage shine in
shadow and light; messenger is black stone

in three phases.

yes:
two wings fold and spearpoint drop to water
to emerge with one silver disc which is four.

chorus silent off behind dune.

33

Harvester two: merlin


at dusk:
a dark silhouette against bright sky comes fast
from treeline into the open. wings flick swift

and low
through
still air:

it is depth of night come to collect that
part of day still clinging at the edge.

it is darkness come
to light, scattering
come to gather.

chorus, annular eyes shut, calls from slumber at the shore:

we.


if messenger at noon is three phases
of black stone, here is another yet:

black moon,
all-crescent,
dark harvest;

*falx mirabilis,* marvelous sickle.

we didn't.

trim wings paddle and body come to hover,
obsidian eye locked to gibbous light below.

wings draw taut and
loose body toward
that faint glow.

we did not.

messenger arrives in brilliant loga-
rithmic swoop dark from above

as sickle in
its gleaming
drop to earth.

dodge the blade once, twice. but it comes
each evening to collect that part still

clinging.

we. we did it.

and when it does, it carries the light
scattered here in the open across tree-

line to sleep
for an interval
beneath that

silent gathering velvet canopy.

# Point phases



eye of goose new in the rushes
wide ● shorn crescent of drift
lit at sunset ◐ quartzite first

quarter in the palm letting in some
light ◑ ternwing bright gibbous
waxing tipped in black ◖ thistle-

bloom full chatoyant face to sun ○
talon of merlin the dark crescent into
bright body ◗ basalt quarter warm

but withal opaque in light waning
◐ crescent scaleshine glint in the
waves ◕ two-circle eye ever new.

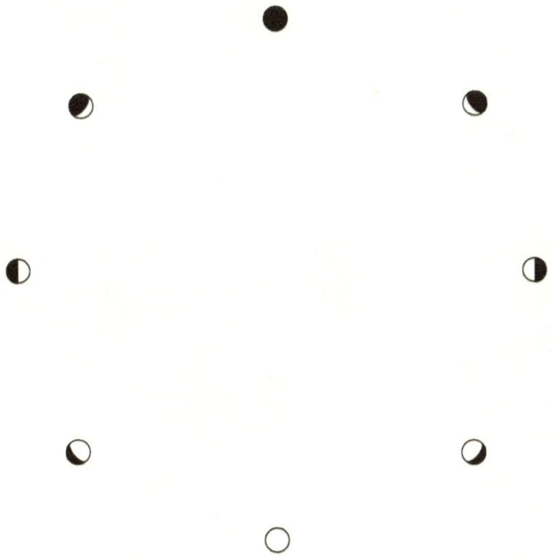

wing is the art-
iculated blade
risen, dividing

quartzite lets in
some light; the
head devours

lit crescent in
projection is
a scattering

where lines join
they return; the
talon gathers

basalt pebble is
the tail devoured
alive and warm

fish is the stone
tool, *lapis*, grasp-
ed and lifted

# Island lines

*14 may ( for white-tailed deer)*

> hoof into
> sandy loam,
> firm connection.
>
> primeval
> swivel,
>
> attention in two
> directions across
> space.

*20 may ( for turkey vulture)*

> wind to
> wing,
>
> flesh
> to flesh
> to soil.

*21 may (for green heron)*

subtle          body

on big          wings

strung    to the bough




*24 may ( for least sandpiper)*

little bird
lock-stich
lake
to shore.

shroud me
in water,
bury me
in sand.

*6 june*

no rest
in the wind

mornings on
the shore shapes
in sand   formed
as I slept,

familiar
images from
beneath.

no rest.

*13 june (for spotted sandpiper)*


duneland artemision, yellow
flowers come; flake    of core-
opsis, fragment    of the disc.

turnstone    don the nightmask,
ring-necked chorus    start to sing:
*roll me    in the stormwash, pluck me*
*from the waves.*

among the temple pillars, sheltered
from the wind, four speckled amber
teardrops    in a ring of woven sedge.

*21 june*


some years
still   and others

not, some sweet and
some in storm; craft

passes   at heart
of night




*5 july (for pitcher's thistle)*


thistlebloom open       to

crescent moon,       vein

of opal       arc from sun

17 *july*                                                                 45


    when it passes, part
    slips through
    and part is held back
    as in a sieve.

    and so
    one is compel-
    led forward
    by the ribs.


24 *july ( for ring-billed gull)*


    two stones placed
    on smoothed sand:

    one, for ivory
    neck, quartzite
    and one, for black
    wingtip, basalt

    wet sand dries
    in the air. *may*
    *you fly again.*

*25 july (for great blue heron)*


pikepoint thrust into fresh
water,     rain breach bank.

kitewings lift just     before
landing, legs long greeting

to sand.       *blind me now,*
               *generous hunter.*

# Anamnesis

1

In the drift is nestled a
granite sphere, at rest.
Long darkness just be-
neath the bright surface.

In it the opposites coincide:
glacier and bedrock, quartz
and iron. Snowblind white
above, dark earth below.

Call it shadow of a blinding god
cast into clear ice, a single point
in ten-thousand-dimensional
space: henahedral stone.

2

Granite sphere splits
along the meridian.
Quartz to east, iron
to west.

It is a body now in
two halves; bright
head and dark tail:
dihedral stone.

Indeed opposites retract. Glacier lifts
from bedrock, shadow is forgotten in
mist; *unless one integrates the other
the whole is nothing.*

3

But when the halves join
and the grains mingle, the
stone's two faces multiply
to ten thousand.

Glacier descends,
body re-forms
beneath the heavy
water of memory;

shadow rises from the mist to full height
and points to where we sit. Call it stone risen
to the likeness of a god, a ten-thousand-
faced body: myriahedral stone.

4

We are the stone.
Call us shadow to god
incarnated to body; we
are many faces to all.

We are the coincidence of opposites,
quartz and iron each, ice pressed
amorous to earth. Long darkness
beneath bright surface. Yes:

head devours tail. We are
the sphere's all-center;
panahedral stone
nestled in drift:

one here
the whole.

# Hymn to phases

Of all the modes of stone

   *sunwarm, rainwet, atop;*
   *out-of-sight, covered, cold*

of all—lit obscure
against black heaven—

you our risen mirror still
the most comprehensible.


        *



Of all the phases

   *molten, solid,*
   *fragmented, flowing*

you our visitor from abroad,
vagabond, traveler,

having passed through each
in your arcane migration—

and each
again.

⁜

And of all the keys of stone

    *to-palm, under-*
    *seat, by-sole*

only the archaic one,
that *before-the-eyes,*

keyed to you our mirror;
glory opposite the sun.


⁜



You of round face!
luminous, *lighting-rites;*

your eyes calm seas
held lenticular

by the dark
body's pull; still

a light come from just
beneath the surface.

# Traveler



Black stone warm      in the winter sun      split as it is
and windworn      spread to lay      as a fossilized body

posed among familiar strata.      Our visitor    along his
way to us    danced beneath the stars   and among signs

numerous and moving    toward    that immortal pose.
The pose      a last long gesture      in the sidereal dance

an asterism      a few last steps taken      before stopping
to lay        down        for a time        out of the wind.

Dog-star marks
the coming flood:

a cord binds the
golden sheaf,

the instrument of
pearl is strung taut

and in the torchlight
our visitor approaches.

Follow arc of thread
from out of the knot,




toward sickle-blade
spinning on flat stone:




a vessel has come down
to water, to raise it,




and alas! the meeting of
cool water and pure torch.

# Artemis in projection

Through the osier glimpse the figure turning
to rise naked from the spring, crescent bow
slung over shoulder.

She may be many-named, this god of the golden
arms, of white wings held aloft and long legs to
earth: called wearer-of-masks, delighting-in-
arrows, strong-voiced, lady of clamors. But no
names now, simply a steep beauty. A stark slope
I would climb endlessly if asked, climb
without rest.

And so hubris rises in the body to settle leaden
at the crown. She turns, eyes like arrows loosed
deft before the gaze, like a bull's horn into the belly,
like intuition. A gaze I crave as much as I fear.

Yes! Swing your golden arms poised so the taut
crescent disappears in profile and the arrow collapses
to a point of light. Yes. It is that cyclopean gaze I
crave, gaze of companion but never lover, gaze like
spring water on the tongue. Yes! I am thirsty.

Now lift hubris from crown and place it on a mossy
trunk beside, to be shot wingbeat quick dead center
from afar. Terror and relief down through the body.

You lifter of weight! Shower me with arrows. Points
generously given, white feathers withheld.

*Drift gestures*

a round and borrowed light,
it whirls about the earth


EMPEDOCLES

# Imbolc



Never more clear than highest winter
under silica bowl rung rare green,

the sun—anyone's great risen god,
anyone's obscure animal set to citrine

—never more clear this sun,
reaper and originator both,

who disappears out beyond ice to-
ward that rumored mirror shore.

# Chorus one: a visitor at the end of winter

She arrives, without fail, when the first green shoots emerge through the snow. But her arrival is no surprise; we've seen the signs, paradoxical as they may be, for some weeks. And we recount them for her:

*White shoulder of deep snow turning,*
*something rising steadily in the veils of flame,*
*black water through thick ice.*

She arrives, folds her wings, and sits quietly beside the hearth, tracing designs in the ashes with her toe. She doesn't demand praise, but still:

*You many-dimensional rise, gentle knoll,*
*you bath of milk, unmoved multiplier—*
*here a brilliant three-faced goddess.*

She leaves at sunset and we rush to the hearth to look at the designs. They make little sense, but we interpret them as best we can. Join us, if you like:

*Circle sunwise, place a coin in the spring,*
*cut the reeds, weave them into four spokes,*
*take some water and sprinkle it round the belly.*

# Equinox



It is a varied plumage that
iridesce from feldspar to um-

ber, from burgundy to lime
peeking from the split bud.

*

Who among us walk a hand-
breadth over the water,

who don the poly-
chromatic mantle?

*

Depth attendant ever
to narrowing, and

plumage weighs
heavy as stone.

# Chorus two: in a rare east wind



After the equinox an east wind blows across the moraine, tumbling backward over dunes and bent pine. Water beads up along waxy blade and the chorus speaks, twelve as one:

> *Call it pliant stem, rising precipitate, thin song,*
> *call it wind-rose, forked branch,*
> *call it gesture.*

Jack pine needles divide the wind into countless streams and it converges again in the lee. A sharp-keeled stone splits the wind in two for a continuous instant. The chorus proceeds:

> *Call it Proteus, arc of spiral, all-center,*
> *call it phasing moon-disc, both-in-each,*
> *call it iridescence..*

The east wind tumbles over the brink and carries out over dark water toward sky. The chorus concludes, equivocally:

> *It is settling air, deep lens, dispassionate gaze,*
> *and while it has no name we know,*
> *it may answer to silence.*

(after Lao Tzu)

Pilgrim (at Beltane)

Finally
the mineral dish

holding this lens
of cold water.

Finally the shore
to hand to feet and

here I sense
that I am two

waves through
one body.

⌗

Even if be-
neath earth

waters join and
all lakes are one

lake
there

still this dish
makes this lens.

⁜

I crouch and run
fingertip to rim

so body tunes to
vessel and two

waves return
to still center.

⁜

But I am not
the center I am

drifting hub
of spokes.

⁜

Still the center
is here.

## Chorus three: apian heathen hof

Just past Beltane, in the marsh behind the ruins, where the line
of maples along the bluff casts long lancet shadows in the low
spring sun, the choir warms its voice.

*Come Antigone, you echo-*
*maker, join the polyphony.*

*Come rising crucible, dayspring,*
*our torpor has been long.*

*Come sweet spring, holy days of*
*nectar, come ponderous priestess.*

Beneath the boughs of apple in soft pink bloom, the apse. Bum-
blebees throw themselves from blossom to blossom, covered
in yellow pollen, seeking nectar. They thrash in their revelry;
here they receive the body and the blood. Phasing staccato swells
arrive from the marsh.

*O echo, o portent,*
*mingle at the base.*

*Teach us the ritual: memory*
*of yet-to-be, bring us fruit.*

*O great serpent, Ouroboros,*
*show us again we are all.*

And beneath the apse, the crypt. Soil rich with fruit and wood,
shed antlers, cellar stones buried, old-country bones. The sun
sets and cool air settles. The new crescent moon is an arc of
a spiral hanging silently over the resonating choir, over the
buzzing apse and the slumbering crypt, up in the darkening
vault of the sky.

> *Praise be to the sun, and to the moon,*
> *and to the ten thousand things.*
>
> *Praise be to disintegration, and to*
> *confluence, and to the recurrent image,*
>
> *as it once was, will be again, and ever*
> *by turns shall be: line with no end.*

# Moebius strip

Around the shore of the island
we walk. Atop saturated drift

to bedrock. Along that
porous pebbled border.

Where flux
and form

two sides of one surface.
We walk. One trip

on the light side. One
in the dark. Awake

we tread on sun-
warm stones. In sleep

soles sink in sand. And
meet. The cool water.

Recurrence one: wing

Lapped sand, wingwash flutter,
mineral once moved
shall return.

Water memory, memory in muscle,
memory in the sandspeckle shell,
crescentic gesture eternal.

Pebble to egg, wind to wing
in flight; recurrence is heavy
but the image is light.

# Toward a principle of iridescence

1    Our movement is circular movement.

2    Our approach is oblique; it follows the circumference, circles the *center*.

3    The center is manifold, possibly everywhere, and our movement loops and veers—so in circling we simultaneously evoke and describe the *spiral of arcs*, which tortuously circles this proposed *omnicenter*.

4    Omnicenter, all-center: a serpent who in its recursive circling might multiply to find tail at every turn.

5    The spiral of arcs is a dance, a dimly apprehended ritual, which is to say both echo and portent at once. We see its arcs appear in the crescent moon, in the redeeming talon of falcon, the elastic catenary of honeybee's flight, in a sliver of shell embedded in stone.

6    The dance is an evocation and description of the border between *seeming opposites:* lightness and weight, ego and other, conscious and unconscious, light and dark.

7    Along the way we encounter the *disc*, which appears in many guises but is known on sight: sun-disc, golden coin, mouth of crucible, great disc of ice floating atop a deep lake, full moon. The disc is an element of the opposite ever present, but often hidden, each side of the border. It is a hint at wholeness, a prompt to *repetition*.

8   Our circular movement is repetitive, and with repetition
    comes the possible reconciliation of the seeming opposites:
    a fleeting apprehension of the both-in-each, a collapse into
    puzzling *unity*.

9   Unity rises, when it does, as a subtle harmonic oblique even
    to our spiraling dance, puzzling in its *iridescence* from blue
    to green to gold before diverging to split once again.

10  Iridescence then is a glimpse of that divine sliver in each,
    a gaze returned.

# Solstice

It slips past in the dark, that tall
walker. That tremendous stride.

It carries beyond pursuit before
we can rise. Even to our feet.

Hematite in the east, a rush of mid-
summer air. Again toward evening.

# Vision (at Midsummer)



Among the perched dunes back from the brink, in a low spot where the body of the moraine is exposed, a basalt erratic. The stone is big, wedged by ice into twelve pieces, worn by wind-blown sand into beguiling forms; worn smooth as raven's beak, black. A sand cherry grows in the midst and a small dune has accumulated in the lee. Press palm to warm stone and receive the vision:

*Transverse face on the horizon, horrible*
*rhombic skew-half, that sculptor and destroyer*
*at once; immanentizer of wholly-new:*

*that which came*
*before and will come*
*inevitably again.*

*Back beyond from vermilion to cinnabar to*
*garnet to graphite, through ice crushing,*
*heaping, melting, lapping;*

*earthtide flood and*
*ebb endless across*
*present shore.*

*Two diamonds spread to form the hexagon,*
*multiply to twelve and grow to prismatic*
*columns bearing down on the polylith;*

*black*
*boulder*
*ascends.*

Recurrence two: arc

Come reconciler hum
your puzzle into air    in-

to muscle    where it
may eddy and hum.

High-summer one
with your enigmatic

hum    turn us round
to face the un-

known part.    If as
you say lightness is

depth and brevity
weight    then

where on the
arc to begin?

Serpent


Loop through the thigh-
bare dunes, press shadow
to till and persist. You
dark remnant through
the meshing gaps.

Persistence called
at the brink. Not as
quality but endeavor
to hold balance on pain
of oblivion. Yes?

Yes but oblivion sweet
and generative too—you
creature less than the stone and
clay of your body—such that
oblivion only a multiplication.

In multiplication head finds
tail at every turn. Tail arrives in
recursive returns fresh each age.
Here as windblown sand, canted
stone, chewing waves.

*What has one voice and ten
thousand feet, but is heard
by no ears? asks serpent.
And still flourishes ever
beyond your puzzling.*

# Swim



this mammal body ever
both sides of the shore

composed as it is of
stone and saltwater

a bit of clay gritty
with ancient shells

and breathed to life
by the waves

# Lughnasadh

On the plateau at dusk, up over the shoulder toward
that fireline guttering orange, orange lifts to green
to still-blue. Over the shoulder see rise the golden disc,
a secret god lifting from the mineral body whose gaze
familiar but startling in its candor.

An intimate image
risen there
to the sky.

Sky blue to obsidian, and below a gleaming lake among
the hills. Still water lit silver against black earth. Moon-
disc, that intimate common come down as round lake
to drift, such that to its shore we might descend and lift
some water in cupped hands.

*Mare cognitum*, sea
that has become
known.

# Equinox



This dark one hidden
beside heart of day

undiscovered yet
drawing still the body

as cottonwood leaves
rattle dry in the wind.

This dark one soon
lit as mineral hook

as arc of luminous spiral
born in late-summer sky

drawing water to rise
to mouth of vessel

that we might each
carry toward fullness.

# Three turns

*One*
Terrible gods-head on the horizon;
turn away—still there, turn away,
can't turn away—turns out all-center.
All-center, reaper and originator as one.

Turning faces, recursion always turning, fractal faces
infernal; iridescence close-in constantly turning faces,
turn away—faces one thought ahead, there already;
no-away. All infernal center in endless turning.

*Two*
How easy to loose the sacred knot; marling-spike
honed slips between and the strands just fall away.
Breath-no-breath, knot to strands into wind.
Wind already there, always there.

*Three*
Lift marl from deepest kettle, mud
from the bed of a flooded footprint,
see a face turning from the water;
spring awaits the golden coin.

# Gesture

shoulder of drift given
beneath shawl
of windblown sand,

blade of grass a compass
wheeling, needle gentle
to bare skin.

eyes climb steep
slope at the vertex of
sense and sensed and

wind sings short
of nothing
through the teeth.

the oracle is continual
and indeterminate
in gesture.

# Samhain

palm to stone
  felt
    through the veil—
thin glinting carapace
    the veil
      before long-dark.

stone
  breathes warmth
    slow.

ochre slurry
    spit
      and stone encases hand—
lift it
  and flesh carries stone,
  only to tumble
    back
      into vertiginous
      living duration.

# Open

flesh flayed open by wave
and the fibres are laid plain.

water through veins of clay to fan
out pulmonary across the sand.

at the shore sacrifice
and sacrificer are one;

here the body
devours the body.

Chorus four: windkanter

When two circles share both center-point and diameter, they
form the disc, the *unus mundus*.

> *What is at once held and withheld,*
> *what in one body thisness and all?*
> *What warmth beneath the sur-*
> *face of a provisional form.*

When the centers diverge and each circumference crosses the
other, one becomes two.

> *Wind scours beneath and*
> *the body tips into the hollow.*
> *A burial. But here too another*
> *face fresh to the wind.*

And finally, when the circles overlap only by the length of the
radius, then a third thing emerges. It is the lens, the *vesica piscis*.

> *Warmth rises to the surface and*
> *all through the body. Stone to wind,*
> *wind to stone. Thisness and all meet*
> *where heat passes to palm. To blood.*

# Return

There is a dense other that pulls, it seems. Why is that?
*There is another body that pulls so you are not flung away.*

If there is a dark other, then who pulls?
*It is Eros that pulls against the cold slope.*

And by what means does it pull?
*It pulls the eyes to sleep and back.*

I am so very tired.
*Let go starry child.*

Your wings, you must be a messenger.
*In sleep each of you alone meets Death.*

Who are you?
*Follow me now.*

# Notes

3    "For souls, death is to become water"
     (Heraclitus, fragment 36, translated by Otto Kern)

12   Unholy Heavenly
     The goddess Aphrodite has many epithets, among them
     *Ourania*, heavenly, celestial; *Pandemos*, for all the people;
     *Androphonos*, killer of men; *Anosia*, unholy.

14   rises in proportion
     "Since energy never vanishes, the emotional energy that
     manifests itself in all numinous phenomena does not cease to
     exist when it disappears from consciousness. As I have said,
     it reappears in unconscious manifestations, in symbolic
     happenings that compensate the disturbances of the conscious
     psyche." (C.G. Jung, *Symbols and the Interpretation of Dreams*
     (CW 18, par. 583), translated by R.F.C. Hull)

14   one unfolds to four
     The axiom of Maria is a principle in alchemy, attributed to
     the third century Alexandrian practitioner Maria Prophetissa,
     which states: "Out of the One comes Two, out of Two comes
     Three, and from the Third comes the One as the Fourth."
     (Marie-Louise von Franz, *Number and Time*, translated by
     Andrea Dykes)

15   just a little water
     "The slight curve of the shell that holds just a little water, just
     a few seeds to give away and to receive, suggests stories of
     becoming-with, of reciprocal induction, of companion species
     whose job in living and dying is not to end the storying, the
     worlding." (Donna J. Haraway, *Staying with the Trouble*)

19   "What was scattered"
(Heraclitus, fragment 40, translated by Brooks Haxton)

25   the first
On one so-called Orphic gold tablet, dating from the fourth
century BCE, we find these instructions for the initiate upon
arriving in the underworld: "You will find to the left of the
house of Hades a spring / and standing by it a white cypress.
/ Do not even approach this spring! / You will find another,
from the Lake of Memory, / cold water pouring forth; there
are guards before it." (Sarah Iles Johnston and Fritz Graf,
*Ritual Texts for the Afterlife*)

32   vociferous
Our chorus here consists of killdeer, *Charadrius vociferus*, a
medium-sized plover so named for its call.

40   Island lines
These poems were composed and spoken aloud during
fieldwork in wind and rain and sun at Point Turnstone on
North Manitou Island. They were transcribed to text only
upon return to the mainland.

49   *unless one*
These lines are paraphrased from Marie-Louise von Franz
(*Alchemy: An Introduction to the Symbolism and the Psych-
ology*) discussing the symbol of the Ouroboros, the serpent
that devours its own tail.

51   one here / the whole
In the *Chrysopoeia of Cleopatra*, a single-page document
attributed to Cleopatra the Alchemist (circa third century
CE) and surviving to us in a tenth century manuscript, the

Ouroboros is depicted surrounding Greek text that reads *hen to pān*, one is the all.

54 among signs
"Only one story of the way is still left: that a thing is. On this way there are very many signs: that Being is ungenerated and imperishable, entire, unique, unmoved and perfect…"
(Parmenides, fragment 8, 1-4, translated by A.H. Coxon)

57 pure torch
"You will know the aether's origin, and likewise all the signs in the aether and the invisible deeds of the pure torch of the brilliant sun, and whence they sprang; and you will learn of the migratory deeds of the round-faced moon and of its origin…" (Parmenides, fragment 9, translated by A.H. Coxon)

63 "a round and borrowed light"
(Empedocles, fragment 52 , translated by Brad Inwood)

65 silica bowl
We owe the image of sky as *mineral bowl* here and elsewhere to the Japanese poet Miyazawa Kenji, as translated by Hiroaki Sato and Gary Snyder.

68 *Call it pliant stem*
We are indebted here to Ursula K. Le Guin's translation of the *Tao Te Ching*, particularly chapter 14, "Celebrating mystery".

70 But I am not
Jung conceives of the *ego* as the focal point of consciousness, the experiencing subject, but not the center of the personality. The ego is a complex that has at its core the archetype of the *Self*, that totality of the personality in its conscious and unconscious portions.

71   *Antigone*
Sandhill crane, *Antigone canadensis*, announces its arrival in
spring with a circling call that echoes among the hills at dusk.

71   *crucible*
Crucible, possibly from the Latin *crux*, cross. The spring
peeper, *Pseudacris crucifer*, is a small chorus frog that bears
an amber cross on its back.

73   Moebius strip
"In our private rest, the restlessness of the cosmos continues
to do its work." (James Hillman, from the introduction to
*Heraclitus: Fragments*)

74   but the image is light
Here we borrow the flight/light rhyme from Michael
Hamburger's translation of Paul Celan's poem with the first
line, "What occurred?"

91   *It is Eros that pulls*
"Eros is inclined towards the beautiful, the appearance of
truth. This is where he differs from pleasure. A time in which
pleasure, the *Like*, is predominant, Heidegger would say, is a
*time without Eros, without beauty.*" (Byung-Chul Han, *Saving
Beauty*, translated by Daniel Steuer)

91   *starry child*
On another Orphic gold tablet, also dating from the fourth
century BCE, the initiate is instructed to declare: "I am a child
of Earth and starry Sky. / My name is 'Starry'. I am parched
with thirst. But grant me / to drink from the spring." (*Ritual
Texts for the Afterlife*)

# Acknowledgements

These poems were written for and among the dunes, waters, shorelines, forests and fields of the Leelanau Peninsula and nearby Manitou Islands between winter 2019 and spring 2022. These places are part of the present, ancestral and future home of Anishinaabe peoples. I thank the Grand Traverse Band of Ottawa and Chippewa Indians for their care for this land, and for allowing me to live and work here.

I invoke the names of the Gaelic seasonal festivals (Imbolc, Beltane, Lughnasadh, Samhain) as a way of reaching back, or fumbling perhaps, along a root of my own ancestry. There are relations there, I imagine, something living in those words. I lay no claim.

To my dear friends and family for their company, and for reading some of the poems as I wrote: my profoundest thanks. And to Kelly, for her parnership in co-creation. All my love.

Special thanks to Joseph Braun and Indigo Deany at the Lune for their generous, perceptive work. A few of these poems first appeared in the journal *Reliquiae*—thanks to Autumn Richardson and Richard Skelton for spotting them over the water.